WORKBOOK

Companion For

Girl, Stop Apologizing

A Shame-Free Plan For Embracing and Achieving Your Goals

By Rachel Hollis

BJ Richards

Notification:

This workbook is based on and meant to accompany the original work by Rachel Hollis, *Girl Stop Apologizing: A Shame-Free Plan For Embracing and Achieving Your Goals*. It is not meant to replace the original work. If you have not read the original work, it is highly recommended you purchase it in conjunction with or prior to using this workbook.

This workbook is meant for educational and entertainment purposes only and has not been authorized, approved, licensed or endorsed by the original book's author or publisher and any of their licensees or affiliates.

All references in this workbook to "Ms. Hollis" or "Ms. Hollis'" are referring to Rachel Hollis, author of *Girl Stop Apologizing: A Shame-Free Plan For Embracing and Achieving Your Goals*.

All references in this workbook to "Ms. Hollis' original work" are referring to Rachel Hollis, author of *Girl Stop Apologizing: A Shame-Free Plan For Embracing and Achieving Your Goals*.

Copyright and Disclaimer

Copyright © 2019, BJ Richards

All rights reserved. No part of this publication may be reproduced, distributed, or transmitted in any form or by any means, including photocopying, scanning, recording, or other electronic or mechanical methods, without the prior written permission of BJ Richards, except in the case of brief quotations embodied in critical reviews and certain other noncommercial uses permitted by copyright law.

Distribution of this book without the prior permission of BJ Richards is illegal, and therefore punishable by law. It is not legal to reproduce, duplicate or transmit any part of this document either in printed format or electronically. It is strictly prohibited to record this publication and storage of the document is not allowed without written permission from the BJ Richards. All rights reserved.

Disclaimer:

Legal Notice: - BJ Richards and the accompanying materials have used their best efforts in preparing the material. This book has been composed with the best intention of providing correct and reliable information. The information provided is offered solely for informational purposes and is universal as so. This information is presented without contract or any type of guarantee assurance.

This workbook is an unofficial summary/analysis/review meant for educational and entertainment purposes only and has not been authorized, approved, licensed or endorsed by the original book's author or publisher and any of their licensees or affiliates.

BJ Richards makes no representation or warranties with respect to the accuracy, applicability, fitness or completeness of the contents of this book. The information contained in this book is strictly for educational purposes and entertainment purposes only. Therefore, if you wish to apply ideas contained in this book, you are taking full responsibility for your actions.

BJ Richards disclaims any warranties (express or implied), merchantability, or fitness for any particular purpose. BJ Richards shall in no event be held liable to any party for any direct, indirect, punitive, special, incidental or other consequential damages arising directly or indirectly from any use of this material, which is provided "as is", and without warranties.

Any and all trademarks, product names, logos, brands and other trademarks featured or referred to within this publication are owned by their respective trademark publications and owners themselves, are not affiliated with this book and are for clarifying purposes only.

BJ Richards does not warrant the performance, effectiveness or applicability of any sites listed or linked to in this book. All links are for information purposes only and are not warranted for content, accuracy or any other implied or explicit purpose.

Recommended Book

I'm sure you already have this, but if not, it's highly recommended you get a copy of the original work, as this workbook is a companion to it.

Girl, Stop Apologizing: A Shame-Free Plan for Embracing and Achieving Your Goals by Rachel Hollis

You can purchase it here: https://www.amazon.com/Girl-Stop-Apologizing-Shame-Free-Embracing-ebook/dp/B07DT7VJ8T

Recommended: Get The Whole Set

The Perfect Journal for This Program:

You're going to need a place to write out your daily steps as you go through the program like: The ten things you're grateful for each day, your intention for the day, tracking your daily habits, notes, etc.

No problem… I have it covered for you! **My journal is designed specifically for the program presented by Ms. Hollis** in her original work, *Girl Stop Apologizing*. This will help you make your journey even easier!

Journal for Girl Stop Apologizing by Rachel Hollis: A Shame-Free Plan for Embracing and Achieving Your Goals by BJ Richards.

The Perfect Planner for This Program:

A planner will be essential to your journey. You'll want a place to set up, track and change your schedule on a weekly, monthly and yearly basis.

I have that covered for you, too! **My planner is designed specifically for the program presented by Ms. Hollis** in her original work, *Girl Stop Apologizing*. This will help you make your journey even easier!

Planner for Girl Stop Apologizing by Rachel Hollis: A Shame-Free Plan for Embracing and Achieving Your Goals by BJ Richards

5 | P a g e
BJ Richards
Workbook Companion for Girl Stop Apologizing by Rachel Hollis

You may also be interested in some of my other books:

1) Find out what coconut oil can really do for you without all the hype. Check out my best-selling book: *Coconut Oil Breakthrough: Boost Your Brain, Burn the Fat, Build Your Hair* by BJ Richards

Check it out here: https://www.amazon.com/Coconut-Oil-Breakthrough-Boost-Brain-ebook/dp/B01EGBA1FW/

2) Do you have a dog? Here's another best seller you may be interested in. You'll find out to deal with a number of issues safely and inexpensively at home. Find out all about it in my best-seller: *Coconut Oil and My Dog: Natural Pet Health for My Canine Friend* by BJ Richards

You can check it out here: https://www.amazon.com/Coconut-Oil-My-Dog-Natural-ebook/dp/B01MUF93U1/

3) Did you know apple cider vinegar and baking soda have some amazing health benefits? Plus, you can use them for so many things in the home and save a ton of money.

You'll find out all about it my boxset: *Apple Cider Vinegar and Baking Soda 101 for Beginners Box Set* by BJ Richards

Check it out here: https://www.amazon.com/Apple-Cider-Vinegar-Baking-Beginners-ebook/dp/B07DPCLWGB/

You can also go **my website** to find even more books I've written and some recommended by other authors: https://bjrichardsauthor.com

Workbook Companion for Girl Stop Apologizing by Rachel Hollis

BJ Richards

Table of Contents

Workbook Companion for Girl Stop Apologizing by Rachel Hollis

Workbook Companion for Girl Stop Apologizing by Rachel Hollis

How To Use This Workbook for Greater Personal Growth

If you're beginner, that's great! My main goal for writing this workbook was so a complete newbie can start to get immediate help in implementing the lessons Ms. Hollis has presented in her book: *Girl Stop Apologizing: A Shame-Free Plan for Embracing And Achieving Your Goals*.

This workbook is as a companion guide to Ms. Hollis' original work and is not meant to replace it. I do recommend you purchase the original work by Rachel Hollis to get the most benefit from this workbook.

You'll find that the chapters are broken down into the following three parts to make it easier for you to implement the steps mentioned is Ms. Hollis' original work. Those parts are:

- Key Points
- Summary / Analysis
- Questions and/or Exercises and/or Worksheets

Key Points: Here I will outline key points I believe were most important in relaying the powerful message presented by Ms. Hollis in the original work.

Summary / Analysis: This is my summarization and analysis of the written content of the chapter.

Questions, Exercises and Worksheets: These are set up to help you personalize and implement the material found in Ms. Hollis' original work. This is done in such a way that you can use these steps and exercises to further develop a clear road map of your own toward your goal and unique personal growth.

BJ Richards
Workbook Companion for Girl Stop Apologizing by Rachel Hollis

You'll find places to write out answers, make lists, brainstorm and take notes as you go along. This will help you keep yourself organized and on track as you work through Ms. Hollis' original work. You'll be able to jot down your ideas and how you want to implement them so you can get started faster and easier with your own goal.

Studies show that writing things out helps to solidify learning. You'll want to keep the workbook handy as you move through your goal process, as the information you write down here will prove to be invaluable as you move along.

Most importantly, the workbook was meant to be fun and aid you in your journey toward self-confidence, happiness and personal achievement.

Enjoy the ride!

Background Story of Rachel Hollis

Rachel Hollis is a modern-day trailblazer for women.

At 27, she was named by INC Magazine as one of the "Top 30 Entrepreneurs under 30". She is founder and CEO of her own media company, Chic Media.

She uses her blog and articles to write about the ups and downs of her own experiences to help other women through the problems in their day-to-day lives. She is living proof that it's hard work and persistence that can make your dream come true, even without a college degree or a lot of money.

Ms. Hollis is a New York Times best-selling author for *Girl Wash Your Face*. She said in an interview she wrote the book because she wanted to help all women everywhere who were dealing with similar issues in their life. She wants to help empower women to overcome the obstacles they encounter and understand they have the power to live their dreams.

Introduction

Key Points:

1. It's your dream. You don't have to justify it.
2. Someone else's opinion is just that, theirs. You don't have to own it.
3. The "what if" you hear calling you is your potential guiding you.
4. Women are still afraid and apologizing for themselves.

Summary/Analysis:

Being you, truly you, is the most valuable thing you can do for yourself and for anyone else. You are unique; you are special. And you have dreams and goals you haven't even begun to explore. Why? Because so many women are living their lives based on someone else's ideas that may not be their own.

So much of a woman's life is tied up in roles they learned as a child. If you're a good mom, then your kids are happy. If you're a good wife, then your husband is content. Almost every woman has been raised with the concept that making the other people around them happy or fulfilled is what makes them a good person.

We were taught to value someone else's opinion about what was good and what was not. How much of your life have you lived based on what other people say or think of you? You want to be accepted so you say the right things to the right people and keep quiet about what you really think so you won't be criticized. You continuously squelch that part of you that needs to be more, to try new things, to evolve and grow.

How many times have you wondered "what if I were to do that". But then you started to question what others would think of your "what if" and worry about their opinion. Or when you talked it over with someone else, they criticized or made fun of your "what if" so that was the end of it. You stopped dreaming.

Women are still afraid of themselves, still apologizing for wanting to pursue their goals and dreams. Still accepting the roles others have deemed correct for them, without giving themselves the chance to move into their own personal growth. That is why Ms. Hollis wrote *Girl Stop Apologizing*. And why this workbook has been written to help you put the lessons from her book to work in your own life.

A true trailblazer, Ms. Hollis has willingly shared her story in her original work to assist women in moving through their own self-imposed roadblocks. She goes into great detail to bring home the point that your dreams are yours, not someone else's. No matter what you do in life, there's someone who's going to criticize you. So get over living your life for someone else's opinion.

She credits her success in achieving her goals to three things:

1. Recognizing the excuses she and others have been stuck in and letting them go.
2. Analyzing her behaviors and habits and adopting new ones that helped her succeed.
3. Learning the additional skills she needed to accelerate her growth.

Her book, *Girl Stop Apologizing*, and this workbook are divided up into those three parts and will become the basis for you achieving your goal, your dream.

It is Ms. Hollis' deep insight and unabashed honesty that has helped women everywhere step out of the shadows and into the light to become all that they can be.

Time for a change.

Workbook Companion for Girl Stop Apologizing by Rachel Hollis

1. What is the "what if" you hear calling you now? Do you hear more than one? List them all.

_____

_____

_____

_____

_____

_____

_____

2. What are the opinions of others you've fallen prey to that stopped you from your "what if"?

_____

_____

_____

_____

_____

_____

3. What is the one area of your life you'd like more help with pursuing and growing into a whole new level?

_____

_____

_____

_____

_____

_____

_____

Workbook Companion for Girl Stop Apologizing by Rachel Hollis

BJ Richards

Part 1: Excuses To Let Go Of

Excuses are anything we hold onto for better or worse that take away our motivation and joy and stop us from living to our full potential. They are set up like roadblocks in our life that we've come to accept and don't even question any more. Until now.

Unfortunately, and unknowingly, we've let those excuses shape our lives and mold us into less than we really could be.

This section will cover some of the biggest excuses that may be holding you back.

Excuse 1: That's Not What Other Women Do

Key Points:

1. Trying to fit in is just another excuse.
2. Pleasing the crowd demands a high price.
3. Accept the challenge of your own "what if".

Summary / Analysis:

This starts early for most us, when we're in grade school. If you weren't one of the "in" crowd you were probably very much aware you were not in the "in" crowd. If you were different, you got teased and laughed at. And you saw those differences as flaws; things about you that were wrong and needed to be fixed. You were different and that was a bad thing.

And rather than be proud of your individuality and the differences that made you unique, you succumbed to other people's opinions. You started trying to fit in and be like them, even if it wasn't who you were on the inside. You led a double life, caught between who you really were and what you needed to be for other people's approval.

Unfortunately, that same pattern followed many women into high school and college, further programming us not to be different or

Workbook Companion for Girl Stop Apologizing by Rachel Hollis

unique. Eventually, we get out of school, get a job and start down the path of becoming an adult. And what have we learned quite well by then? Fit in, be accepted, do what will get you the most praise from your peers, family and society.

How much of the time do we beat ourselves up in our head? For "saying the wrong thing" because it was our opinion and not what we were supposed to say? And what do we learn to do? We learn to criticize ourselves all day for being too fat, too thin, too short, too stupid and on and on and on. That little voice is constantly tell us there's something wrong that needs to be fixed so we can fit in.

We shame and guilt ourselves into roles that we think will be acceptable. And the words "I'm sorry" become a normal part of lives as we constantly apologize for being who we are.

And we not only apologize with words, we apologize with how we act and how we live. Always making sure we stay within the norm so as not to be criticized for getting outside the box. We may be doing it in the way we dress, how we wear our hair or where we go.

And the truth is, a lot of that still comes from what we were taught when we were growing up.

We've had it so ingrained in us that if we're to be a "good" person we need to be accepted by others, and do what we're told is the right thing by someone else's standards. Which means, we're letting someone else determine our self-worth, diminish our self-esteem and act as our judge and jury.

The truth is, you don't have to apologize for being who you are. You have the right to pursue your goals, your dreams and your ambitions. And you can say "no" to that little voice constantly criticizing you.

If you're reading this book, then chances are you've already started to feel there was something else out there for you; that the norms of society were becoming too uncomfortable. You want to spread your wings and grow because there's something inside of you that says, "yes you can". You hear the "what if".

It isn't easy to stop listening to that voice from the past; the one that keeps telling you to just be quiet and fit in. But it is possible. It takes work and it takes a commitment. It's a challenge. But if you pursue the challenge to grow, the possibilities are endless.

1. What are the excuses that have held you back until now?

_____
_____
_____
_____
_____
_____

2. How has your childhood and background impacted who you are today?

_____
_____
_____
_____
_____
_____

3. What are you dreams? The big ones, the middle-sized ones, even the small ones.

_____
_____
_____
_____
_____
_____
_____

Excuse 2: I'm Not A Goal Oriented Person

Key Points:

1. A goal is a dream you've committed to.
2. You have to believe you can be more.
3. You need to have a plan.

Summary / Analysis:

Many women today do not understand what it means to set a goal. It's been something they've heard others talk about, but never related it to themselves. Setting a goal seemed like something far away and difficult and, well, just not who they are.

I'd venture to say a lot of us fit into this category. We really don't understand the whole "goal" thing, don't really know how to go about it and don't see ourselves as that type.

It seems too pushy, too driven, too competitive and just not you. But in reality, having a goal means we have a focus on something we'd really like to accomplish.

We may not accomplish it today or tomorrow or even next year. There are baby steps in everything. But the first step is in understanding what that goal is.

Workbook Companion for Girl Stop Apologizing by Rachel Hollis
BJ Richards

Maybe it's the kind of person you want to be. Or the kind of job you'd like to have. You dream about becoming a writer, or a painter, or traveling abroad. But you haven't done anything about it.

So how does a goal fit into all that? A goal is just a dream that became a purposeful daily effort. Something you've chosen to work toward that makes you smile when you think about it, that gives you motivation. It's something you consciously commit to, plan out and go for.

Many women make the mistake of thinking that if they're a mom they can't have a personal goal for themselves. After all, personal growth would be selfish wouldn't it? Shouldn't your kids and your husband be more important?

You can be an individual and still be a great mom and a great wife. It's okay to make choices that are for your own personal growth and development. The reality is, by accepting the challenge to become all that you can be, you're setting an example for your kids, your family and the world. You're showing them it can be done if they choose to work and make it happen.

But you have to believe it. You have to grab hold and not become complacent. You have to look yourself in the mirror every day and congratulate yourself for showing up.

Goals need a plan. Why? Because they're usually not little things. Little things you do every day without even thinking about them. You decide to you'd like Chinese food, so you go out to dinner. Definitely not a goal.

Goals need to be mapped out. You can't just sit around thinking and not acting; that won't get you anywhere. If you want to learn to draw you need to do something about. It takes action. You have to pick up a pencil and a paper and start making lines and sketches on the paper. You go to YouTube and start watching videos on how to shade and contour. You start taking classes and going to museums and art shows. You read about other artists and what they did and plan out how you can do it, too.

Sure, at first your drawings may look like stick people. But eventually you start to see shapes emerge that actually look like something. You start blending colors you never even knew you understood. Why? Because you mapped out the steps ahead of time and knew where you were going and how to get there. And then you took action.

1. Do you feel you are a goal-oriented person? Why or why not?

_____
_____
_____
_____
_____
_____

2. What are your beliefs that may be holding you back from achieving a goal?

_____
_____
_____
_____
_____
_____

3. Look back at the list of dreams you made in the previous lesson. Prioritize them here in order of most importance to you.

_____
_____
_____
_____
_____
_____
_____

Workbook Companion for Girl Stop Apologizing by Rachel Hollis

Excuse 3: I Don't Have Time

Key points:

1. You don't find the time, you make the time.
2. You need to take charge of your weekly schedule.
3. You must treat your goal hours as sacred.
4. Set your goal hours for when you're sharpest.
5. Every week-end sit down and plan the next week.

Summary / Analysis

I'm guessing this is the most identifiable excuse everyone has. We feel so pulled in multiple directions all day long, the idea of "one more thing to do" just about sends us into a frenzy.

So the point is, you have to make the time; not find the time.

It isn't going to happen if you don't make it happen. This is probably the biggest excuse used for not accomplishing anything. Everything that you're doing right now, you did, not someone else. We put things in our lives. We have children, we go to school, we work extra hours. We make the schedule for our lives. And we can't blame the other guy for it, either.

What it takes is you being willing to trade your time for something you want. That's it. So let's start in.

BJ Richards
Workbook Companion for Girl Stop Apologizing by Rachel Hollis

Part one.

Below is a chart with hours for each day. You're going to use that chart to record what you do in your daily life. And you're going to keep that record for a week. This will show you where your time is going and what you can change to get closer to your goal.

For instance, if you went to the grocery store to shop for an hour, write it down. You took 45 minutes to get ready in the morning, write that down. It's like keeping track of what you eat, but we're doing it with what you do.

I've included a Time Diary for you to use. You can use a regular notebook if you need more space.

My Time Diary

MONDAY

- [ ] _____
- [ ] _____
- [ ] _____
- [ ] _____
- [ ] _____

TUESDAY

- [ ] _____
- [ ] _____
- [ ] _____
- [ ] _____
- [ ] _____

WEDNESDAY

- [ ] _____
- [ ] _____
- [ ] _____
- [ ] _____
- [ ] _____

THURSDAY

- [ ] _____
- [ ] _____
- [ ] _____
- [ ] _____
- [ ] _____

FRIDAY

- [ ] _____
- [ ] _____
- [ ] _____
- [ ] _____
- [ ] _____

SATURDAY

- [ ] _____
- [ ] _____
- [ ] _____
- [ ] _____
- [ ] _____

SUNDAY

- [ ] _____
- [ ] _____
- [ ] _____
- [ ] _____
- [ ] _____

NOTES

- [ ] _____
- [ ] _____
- [ ] _____
- [ ] _____
- [ ] _____

Workbook Companion for Girl Stop Apologizing by Rachel Hollis

BJ Richards

Have you done that for an entire week? Good. Now the next step. You're going to take your first step toward your goal. Feels exciting doesn't it?

Start looking at the Time Diary you just created and decide how you can come up with 5 hours. Don't freak out here. It doesn't have to be one big 5-hour chunk. Think of it as 30 minutes here, an hour there, you get the idea.

Use a different colored pen or a highlighter for this. You want to see just where those minutes are and make them stand out.

Remember, you're making a commitment to you. A five-hour-a-week commitment to yourself. You can do this.

If you have more than five hours in your schedule to commit to yourself and your goal, that's wonderful. Do more. But five hours is the minimum.

Ready, set, go! Get out that colored pen and start planning those five hours. They will become your new habit. And that habit will help get you to your goal.

After you've found them, write those times down in the My Weekly Goal Hours chart. In column one under "Day", write down the day of the week that specific chunk of time is. In the next column labeled "Time Allotted", write down the amount of time. In the third column labeled "From When to When", write down the specific time slot.

For example in the "Day" column you might have: Monday.

And in the "Time Allotted" column you might have: 1 hour.

In the "From When to When" column you might have: 6 – 7 A.M.

Workbook Companion for Girl Stop Apologizing by Rachel Hollis

My Weekly Goal Hours

Day	Time Allotted	From When to When

Workbook Companion for Girl Stop Apologizing by Rachel Hollis

BJ Richards

Part Two. Making your five hours your sacred space.

This is where the rubber meets the road. Where you commit to turning something you've sketched out on paper into a physical thing you do. It's up to you to make the dream you have for yourself more important than your girlfriend calling last minute to invite you to coffee, or your favorite show coming on with the next episode you're dying to see. If you can't make your goal more important that your excuses, then what's the point of doing any of this?

You have to decide. Are you going to keep your schedule and pursue your goal and a better you? Or let others keep you where you are and stop you from becoming who you truly want to be?

Part Three: These are your minimum hours, so make them your best.

You want to be at the top of your game when you're planning your five goal-oriented hours. After all, this is the time you're using to become the new you. If it's easier for you to concentrate in the morning, then try to schedule yours during that period of time when you feel the freshest. Or maybe it's easier at night when the kids are in bed and the house is quiet. Whatever it is, schedule those hours into your day when you have the most focus and your brain hasn't turned to mush. If you have to, go back to your schedule and move things around.

Part Four: You have to plan your weekly schedule.

There's no way around it. Sit down with your significant other if you have one, and go over your schedules together. A good time to do it is on the week-end, so you can look at what's coming up the following week. Don't leave anything out.

Will you have to move your sacred hours around sometimes? Probably. Life happens. You may have to shift them a little time-wise or maybe even to a different day. As much as you want to plan your schedule out for an entire month ahead, it just isn't going to happen that way. So you'll need to be flexible but still be focused and determined.

Think about where you are and where you want to be. You're probably where you are because you were waiting for that special moment to act or do or be. And where has that gotten you?

You need to ask yourself: If not now, then when?

BJ Richards

Workbook Companion for Girl Stop Apologizing by Rachel Hollis

Excuse 4: I'm Not Enough To Succeed

Key Points:

1. You have to give yourself a chance to try.
2. Mental sabotage will stop you from starting.
3. You have to be flexible and adjust as you go along
4. Give yourself credit for the things you've done.
5. Don't let someone else's opinion become your excuse.

Summary / Analysis:

This is a big one and it plagues almost everyone. Not being enough comes in a variety of different packages: I don't have enough money, I don't have enough education, I'm too fat, I'm too thin, I not old enough, I'm not young enough. You get the idea.

You've mentally sabotaged yourself before you ever started. You kept yourself in the same place because it was comfortable, and you didn't want to get out of your box. By being "not enough" you've taken away all you hoped for.

But the truth is, there are thousands of people who made their way through their own "not enough" excuses. And they did it one step at a

Workbook Companion for Girl Stop Apologizing by Rachel Hollis

time. It only seems impossible because you haven't tried to take the first step. Or you took that first step and fell down and didn't pick yourself back up. Toddlers learn to walk because they pick themselves back up after they fall. And eventually they go from walking to running. They keep trying until they get it right.

Keep in mind that this is a personal journey. This is not a one-size-fits-all tee-shirt. Think of it like shopping for a great pair of jeans. You keep trying on different pairs until you find the one that fits.

It's like that. You're going to try different things. Not all of them will work and that's okay. When one doesn't work, you'll try another. And if you have to, you'll try another. And you'll be so focused and determined to succeed, you won't let a couple of oopsies stop you. You're looking for flexible, but firm.

You can either use failure as a learning tool, or you can let it dictate your self-esteem.

So again, do what works for you in your trial and errors.

One very powerful exercise you can do is to write a letter to yourself. You're going to write about the things you accomplished even though you had problems. You're going to write from your courage and your strength and your will to overcome.

Use this letter to give yourself credit for all the things you've been through you never really acknowledged. Write about the things you did someone else couldn't do. You were great in sports or cooking or sewing.

Maybe you lived through a difficult childhood or a bad relationship. Maybe you had almost no money and still got through the storm. Or you got your kids through a terrible night or illness. Give yourself credit for all the little things you've done. Give yourself credit for your strength.

BJ Richards
Workbook Companion for Girl Stop Apologizing by Rachel Hollis

You will use this letter to remind yourself of who you really are inside, not the lies you've been telling yourself. You're going to write from your gut and give voice to your tenacity, your perseverance, your heart. Use the space here to do it right now.

Letter To Myself

_____

_____

_____

_____

_____

_____

_____

_____

_____

_____

_____

_____

_____

_____

_____

_____

_____

_____

So what's the take away? All those excuses end up being an opinion. Someone else's opinion you've grabbed onto because it spoke to one of your insecurities. Maybe it came from an authority figure like a parent or teacher. Or maybe from your peers constantly teasing you. Regardless, they are someone else's opinion of what or who you could become. Nothing more.

You've opened your eyes now. You can recognize those excuses for lies and opinions and nothing more. If you can do that, you stop letting them control you. You can move forward into a better brighter you.

1. Make a list of all the "I'm not enough" excuses you've given power to.

_____
_____
_____
_____
_____
_____

2. Which of those things you just listed has been your biggest roadblock?

_____
_____
_____
_____
_____
_____

3. Now write down 5 things you can do to break that excuse apart and build a whole new habit to help you keep your goal. Make this practical.

_____
_____
_____
_____
_____
_____
_____

Workbook Companion for Girl Stop Apologizing by Rachel Hollis

Excuse 5: I Can't Pursue My Dream and Still Be a Good Mom/Daughter/Employee

Key Points:

1. There's no such thing as balance between work and your personal life.
2. If you stay centered, everything else will pull itself together.
3. Your health and well-being needs to be first in your list of priorities.
4. Don't let the mommy-guilt monster eat you alive.

Summary / Analysis:

This is one of those fill-in-the-blank excuses. Maybe it's "sister" instead of "mom". Or "wife" instead of "mom". The excuse is the same, regardless of which one it is.

We may have used this excuse subconsciously for years. You don't take that art class you've been talking about because your husband would have to cook dinner for everyone and watch the kids. So you give up on your dream of expanding your artistic abilities. Or you turn down a great job because it would mean moving to the next town and your parents would feel they're being abandoned. So you stay put working in a job you only tolerate to pay the bills.

We tell ourselves a good mom or good daughter wouldn't do that. So we stay stuck. And that can lead us to bitterness and resentment. And then we dislike ourselves even more because we feel guilty for that.

Which brings up the whole work/life balance issue. We've been told if you can't balance both equally, you're not doing it right. Which means you're being a poor employee or mom or wife.

The truth is, it's a trade-off. You may have to miss some family time in order to pursue your dream. You may have to take time off work to take the kids to the dentist. It will shift back and forth because that's just life. So don't let the opinion that it must all be in perfect balance all the time make you believe you're less than. Because you're not.

Instead, the goal is to be centered. If you stay centered, then everything else will come off as it should. And that means taking care of yourself.

The scales move back and forth around a pivot point. Sometimes there's more weight on one end and sometimes it goes the other way. In the end, it all comes back to center. Which brings us back to the previous point. If you stay centered, it doesn't matter which way the scales go, because you're grounded and calm inside.

So don't let someone else make your life choices. Don't listen when they tell you it's one or the other and there's no in-between. Maybe it's their opinion, but it doesn't have to be your reality.

What about your priorities? Where do you stand compared to your relationship, the kids, work? Have you put yourself first, second, third? To some it's almost heresy to say you have to put yourself first, then everything else after that, but it's true. If you're sick and so harried all the time you can barely think, how well can you really help your kids, or do your job, or contribute to your relationship. Stop and think about it for a minute. When you feel fabulous, doesn't everything else flow much easier? Even on the airlines they tell the adults to put their oxygen mask on first. Because if the parents can't breathe, how can they help their children get their masks on?

The other biggee affecting almost every mother out there is guilt; specifically mommy guilt. It's that nasty little voice in your head that says "A good mom would do this. A good mom wouldn't have done that."

And we let it fester and eat away at our hearts and our minds until we question everything we've ever done, how we did it and why. That's crazy! You made the best choice you could at the time for your children. Mommy guilt is one of the least constructive things we can put ourselves through. When that ugly monster rears its head, stop and ask yourself, "Did I do the best I could at the time with the knowledge and resources I had then?" And you know what? The answer will invariably be "yes".

1. Do you feel you are centered and calm inside? Yes or no. Explain why.

_____
_____
_____
_____
_____
_____

2. What are the top 3 things that are keeping you off-center and ungrounded?

_____
_____
_____
_____
_____
_____

3. List your priorities and why you have them in that order. Where are you on that list? Are you first? Where is your relationship, kids, work?

_____
_____
_____
_____
_____
_____

Excuse 6: I'm Terrified Of Failure

Key Points:

1. Keep your dreams alive and don't give up.
2. Failure is nothing more than a lesson to be learned
3. If you're going to succeed, you have to stick it out.
4. You have to look at every failure as the door to a new opportunity.

Summary / Analysis:

Do you have a dream you've always thought about? But it seemed so impossible all you ever did was think about it? And you were too embarrassed to talk about it or share it because it was just too far out there?

You can still get there if you accomplish the smaller dreams that lead up to it. Set smaller goals and accomplish those first. Let those successes drive you forward to the big impossible dream you keep close to your heart.

It doesn't happen overnight. It's going to take time and focus and courage. And you're going to need to understand there are going to be failures along the way, a lot of them. But you to have to pick yourself up and dust yourself off after each and every one of those failures.

Workbook Companion for Girl Stop Apologizing by Rachel Hollis
BJ Richards

You have to not be embarrassed because others saw you fail. Other people's opinions can be very powerful if you let them. But they're only an opinion. You don't have to accept it. You don't have to live your life by it.

Let them see you fail and stand back up. Let them see what real determination looks like. Eventually they're also going to see you succeed and that will be grand!

It's important you start to look at failures as lessons. Start picking them apart to see what they're really made of. Sure, you may have blown the whole thing in the end, but what did you develop along the way that you can turn into a positive to help you move forward?

Maybe you tried desperately to lose 30 pounds. But every time you got to the half-way mark you relapsed and went right back into your old eating habits. But when you go back and really look at what happened you realize it was one specific emotional trigger that started your spiral down. And you never realized that before because you were so busy beating yourself up, you never stopped to truly analyze what happened.

Knowing that one key piece of information is huge! Because that's something you can work on and get help for. That's something you can heal. Which means the next try will have a completely different outcome.

Perseverance is everything. People succeed because they pushed through the hard times and picked themselves up after they fell. Life is trial and error. You're going to win some and you're going to lose some. But when you win, it feels awesome because you earned it.

Be grateful for the times when you felt insecure. They helped you figure out what makes you comfortable and at peace. Don't hate yourself because you can only afford to live in a small place. It teaches you to be not be wasteful and get creative with what you have. Every less than perfect situation presents an opportunity to grow and develop in a whole new way.

Start to treat life's failures as new opportunities to grow. Because those are not really failures. True failure is when you give up and stop trying. True failure is when you let other people's opinions stop you from even starting.

1. What are the failures and insecurities you've felt the strongest about.

_____
_____
_____
_____
_____
_____

2. Why did you feel so bad about them? Were other people's opinions involved? Whose and why did that matter so much?

_____
_____
_____
_____
_____
_____

3. Knowing what you know now, what lessons can you get from them? How can you turn that into a growth opportunity?

_____
_____
_____
_____
_____
_____
_____

Workbook Companion for Girl Stop Apologizing by Rachel Hollis

Excuse 7: It's Been Done Before

Key Points:

1. Comparing yourself to others can stop you before you start.
2. There is nothing that hasn't been done before, but you can put a new spin on it.
3. Learn to use someone else's success as inspiration.
4. Get clear about your why.

Summary / Analysis:

This excuse is so common it's sad. We tell ourselves someone else already did it, so why even try. But did you let that stop you from wearing the latest fashion or getting married or going on a date? Of course not!

You'd be pretty hard pressed to think of anything that hasn't been done before. We just use "it's already been done" as an excuse because we're afraid we'll fail… miserably. And then people will laugh at us and we'll feel even worse. But if we don't even try it, then we can't fail and avoid all that misery to start with. You've started out with such a negative mindset you can't even see the starting gate.

You're not going to be perfect to start with. No one is.

You look at someone who's killin' it and tell yourself you could never do it that well… ever. They already have it nailed and everyone knows it.

What if we turned that around. What if we looked at someone else's success as an inspiration instead of a deterrent? You see Janie has made a great side income with her alterations & sewing. Maybe you could make a little side cash selling those cute earrings you make at a craft fair.

Comparing yourself to the next guy in a negative way is lose-lose. Not only are you telling yourself you're not enough, you're telling yourself you never will be so why even bother.

You're saying you need to start out the gate at the same success level someone else has attained after years of hard work. And I'm guessing if you knew their story, you'd find out they started with nothing and felt just like you're feeling right now.

Are you going to be bad at something in the beginning? Probably. Could you write the alphabet the first time you picked up a pencil? No. But you're aces at it now. Because you kept trying and doing until you did it.

Almost anything can be learned. And that includes your dream… your goal. So decide right now if you're okay with not being perfect in the beginning to get to where you want to be. If you say that's asking too much, then you're going to stay right where you are.

It's all about your fears. Are you holding yourself back because you think you'll be humiliated? Or you don't know what you're doing? Or you've failed before so why is this different? These are excuses. Excuses to be let go of.

I guarantee you, every issue and excuse you've held onto that has stopped you, the people you're comparing yourself to went through at some point also. The difference is they tried anyway. And they did it their way. And so can you.

You've got a dream, a goal. Stop and think about why you want it. How will it make you feel, what will it help you accomplish as a person, how will that impact your future and your self-esteem? Your why is your motivation. You need to feel it in your gut. You need to be clear about your why.

Workbook Companion for Girl Stop Apologizing by Rachel Hollis

1. Is there someone you've compared yourself to? What are the qualities they have you wish you had?

_____
_____
_____
_____
_____
_____

2. Now think about that person you were comparing yourself to. What can you learn from that? How can you use their footsteps to create an even bigger and better path of your own.

_____
_____
_____
_____
_____
_____

3. What is your why? Why do you want this goal? What makes it important and gets you buzzing?

_____
_____
_____
_____
_____
_____
_____

Workbook Companion for Girl Stop Apologizing by Rachel Hollis

Excuse 8: What Will They Think?

Key Points:

1. Judgmental people will judge you no matter what you do.
2. Non-judgmental people will be supportive.
3. You get stronger when you ignore the jerks.
4. Don't confuse an honest opinion with approval.
5. You must stay true to who you are.

Summary / Analysis:

Let's face it. People love to gossip. And if they can't find anything solid to gossip about, they'll make up a half-truth and go with that. Those types of people are judgmental; there's nothing you can do about them and no reason to care about what they say. They're dealing with their own issues of who knows what and you really don't want to step into the middle of that. And honestly, no matter what you do, they're going to talk about it behind your back. You have to decide if you're going to let that type of person control who you are and what you accomplish.

Then there are the non-judgmental types. The ones who try new things and who encourage others to do the same. They aren't going to talk about you because you've failed at something. They're doing their best and have their own failures, too. They understand life is full of ups and

Workbook Companion for Girl Stop Apologizing by Rachel Hollis
BJ Richards

downs and in-betweens and are too busy living their own life to judge yours.

The fear of doing something others will disapprove of is a big one. It can hold you back from you dreams because the thought of being laughed at and gossiped about is just too embarrassing for some. The truth is, no matter what you do they're going to laugh and talk because they're just that kind of person. Many of those people are they're so unfulfilled and insecure, they're too afraid to do anything that puts them out there. So they take it out on those they see with the courage to step forward and fulfill their dreams.

Once you stop letting what someone else says or thinks about you determine your actions, life becomes easier and you get stronger. Why does it get easier? Because you're not wasting your mental and emotional energy worrying about pleasing the crowd instead of accomplishing your goal. Instead, all that time and energy goes into your life, your happiness and the satisfaction you're doing something important for you.

You don't need those people to bounce ideas off of. You will hopefully have true friends or family for that or someone else in the community you respect and can talk to. Someone who is also living their life with value and purpose.

Just be careful you're really asking for an opinion and not for someone's approval. There's a fine line of distinction between how you interpret what someone else has to say and what you do with it. Are you asking for someone's opinion because you truly want another point of view? Or are you really seeking their approval?

You must stay true to who you are. You must have that firmly imbedded in your heart and your gut. Other people's opinions will steal away your power.

Remember, it's your goal and your dream. It's your enthusiasm and your focus that will keep you focused and keep you flying high. Don't let someone else's opinion shoot an arrow through your balloon. You'll end up deflated and flat instead of soaring with the eagles.

1. Who are the people you can go to if you want another point of view who will not judge you?

_____
_____
_____
_____
_____
_____

2. What intentional steps can you take going forward to keep you focused on your truth and not other people's opinions?

_____
_____
_____
_____
_____
_____

3. What image do you have of yourself right now? How do you see yourself in the future?

_____
_____
_____
_____
_____
_____
_____

Excuse 9: Good Girls Don't Hustle

Key Points:

1. You can hustle and still be a good mom and wife.
2. There's a difference between gratitude and blind acceptance.
3. You can have it if you're willing to work for it.

Summary / Analysis:

Being an over-achiever is not bad. Wanting to do something because it makes you feel good is not bad. Accomplishing something people around you haven't, isn't bad. Yes, you can hustle and still be a good mom and wife.

Society's role for the hustlers has been the men… the achievers, the "big guns". And not only is it okay for men to hustle, it's expected of them. But girls were taught to go after the boys. Be their wife and raise their children. Yes, you could work as a woman. But you had to make sure you husband and your kids came first. Hustling was being pushy, and women aren't supposed to make that kind of a statement, because that's impolite.

So you grew up knowing there was a difference between the girls and the boys. The boys went out into the world and blazed the trails, and the girls followed and supported them. You were told to be satisfied and be grateful for what you got.

But being grateful and just blindly accepting anything that comes along are two different things. It's okay to want more than you have, but still be grateful for the things in your life.

It's okay to hustle, to set personal goals, to let the world know you're there and can contribute more than they thought.

Stop and think about it. If you never set new goals for yourself, if you never strive to be more, where is your life going? If you're not growing as a person what are you doing? How can you be helping others if you won't help yourself?

Does that mean that stay-at-home-moms aren't really working? Oh, please! That's one of the hardest jobs on the planet. But not every woman is cut out for it just because they're not made that way. You may love your husband and your kids, but you may not be able to be around them 24/7 without going crazy.

So, can you still be a good mom and wife and still be a great employee or career gal? Of course you can! Can you be a stay-at-home-mom and still hustle and make your goal a reality? Absolutely!

Hustling is going for it. It's working toward it. It's stepping forward into your power and not letting other people's opinions get in the way. It means you're willing to work for it and get through the challenges even when it's hard.

It all comes down to this. A better you is a better mom, better wife, better employee, better world. But it starts by making a better you first.

1. What are the things you're grateful for?

_____
_____
_____
_____
_____
_____

2. What would you like to make a reality in your life you'd be willing to hustle for?

_____
_____
_____
_____
_____
_____

3. What are your unique talents and how can you use them to get you through the challenges as you pursue your goal?

_____
_____
_____
_____
_____
_____

Workbook Companion for Girl Stop Apologizing by Rachel Hollis   BJ Richards

Part II: Behaviors To Adopt

Behaviors are nothing more than our habits. Things we've learned to do or have been trained to do over time. We do them automatically without even thinking about them. But at one time we made a choice to do them. And if we made a choice to do them, we can make a choice to undo them.

It's the same for our beliefs. At one time we chose to believe something. Which means if that belief is no longer working for us, we can choose to change that belief or disregard it completely.

You've done a great job working through all the excuses and why you're not going to let them control you anymore. So now we're going to cover behaviors to help you get to your goal.

Behavior 1: Stop Asking Permission

Key Points:

1. You've outgrown your need for someone else's permission.
2. Asking permission takes away your power.
3. You have the right to choose your joy and pursue it.

Summary / Analysis:

This is not about the boys vs. the girls. This chapter may sound "feminist" to you, but don't get the wrong idea. There is no crusade here against men. What is being pointed out is that some of those values you were taught growing up need to be considered. Why? Because they may still be affecting your belief in yourself. And that affects your goal.

This chapter is all about the height of personal growth and overcoming years of training almost all women have had since they were born… accepting the decisions of the authority figure in their life. Most probably it was your father. Whatever he said was the rule. That's just how it was.

And like most children you probably wanted to please your parents and seek their approval. Everyone wants to hear "good job" every now and then. But if we don't transition past that in our adult lives, then we're still seeking permission from an authority figure. And if the main authority figure in your life growing up was your father or a man, then you may still be asking permission as an adult from your husband or boyfriend.

And that takes away the power you need to accomplish your goals. If we as women can't learn to think on our own and make our own decisions without having another person tell us whether or not those decisions are right or wrong, we're giving away our power.

Don't take this the wrong way. No one is saying do whatever you want with no consideration for the other person in the relationship. What is being said is make your decisions based on good sound judgment and don't ask permission from your partner if it's okay.

Think about all the things you do that are really asking permission. Like "I'd like to run to the store if you're okay with that." Or, "Do you mind if I go to the movies Tuesday night with Cheryl?" You're asking someone else's permission when you do that.

What can you change in your behavior about that? Maybe turn it around to, "I'm going to the store. Be back in a minute. Do you need anything?" You're not asking anyone's permission. And you're not making an enemy of your partner. Your relationship is important to you and you want it to be win-win.

It's important to your self-esteem that you're proud of who you are as an individual. You want it to show in the way you walk, the way you talk, the way you carry yourself. Your self-belief has everything to do with your inner strength and your determination to succeed. And that has everything to do with your commitment to your future and your goal.

1. What kind of woman do you want to be? Who do you really want to see when you look at that image in the mirror?

_____

_____

_____

_____

_____

_____

2. Think about the values you were brought up with as a child. Were you taught to value your own opinion and think for yourself? What were you taught?

_____

_____

_____

_____

_____

_____

3. How are those same values still affecting you today? Is there anything about that you'd like to change?

_____

_____

_____

_____

_____

_____

Workbook Companion for Girl Stop Apologizing by Rachel Hollis

Behavior 2: Choose One Dream and Go All In

Key Points:

1. If you focus on more than one goal, you'll get overwhelmed.
2. You need a ten-year plan.
3. Know your ten dreams.
4. Choose only one goal at a time.

Summary / Analysis:

We've all learned to multi-task. That term is extremely common, and often times necessary in order to survive in the world.

But when we're talking about a goal, it's not where you want to be. You want all your energy focused and determined toward one main accomplishment. One, not two or three. Why? Because it takes the power and energy away from the most important one you're trying to achieve.

Yes, you probably have a whole list of things you'd like to do. And that's great. But there's a difference between great ideas and dreams.

A dream is something you have a real desire for. That one thing that makes you smile every time you think about it. That causes that excited buzzing feeling in your gut. That's a dream. That's different from great ideas. The ideas are good, but they don't give you the buzz, the silent inner rush you get from thinking about your dream.

Now I know some of you may be saying you don't know if you have a dream. But you're going to find there's one thing you think about that gets the buzz going and brings the smile to your face.

That one dream, the one with the strongest buzz, is going to be your goal for right now. There will be other goals after that, but this is where you start.

By starting out with only one goal there's nothing else to distract you. You're focused, determined and not bailing out on it by starting another project and taking away your much-needed time, energy and resources from it. If you do that, you'll get overwhelmed and quit. So one goal at a time.

This is about personal growth. Your personal growth. You have a life away from your dream that has nothing to do with it. Kids, a partner, family, work. So when you carve those sacred hours out of your schedule, you don't want to get lost in the shuffle. One goal at a time. And accomplishing just that one goal will spill over into everything else in your life. When you grow and evolve, everything around you grows and evolves. It's like magic.

Ms. Hollis likes to use her 10/10/I process to help her decide on her goal. This is what she says to ask yourself.

1. Who do you want to be in 10 years?
2. What are the ten dreams that would make that a reality for you?
3. Which one of those dreams are you going to turn into a goal to focus on next?

Start with question number one: Who do you want to be in 10 years?

1. Write it out in detail: Who do you want to be in 10 years. Be specific. What do you look like? Where are you living? What clothes do you wear? Where do you live? What does your house look like? How do you feel about the people around you and how they do feel about you? Are you single, married, are there kids in the picture? Take your time and write this out in detail. Have fun with this.

2. Now take that and go even deeper. What kind of work do you do? Or do you work and what happens to you because of that? Think about your values. What drives you in that world? What ignites your passion? This is not the time to be sensible or start judging your list. Just write down everything that comes into you head. Want to make it even more fun? Make yourself a vision board. Cut out pictures of all the things you've imagined and put it on there. Cut out the words you see yourself as for values and put those on the board. Now you can see it represented in living color in front of you. This is a very powerful step.

Take the time to do that now before moving on. You can use the space provided for you here to answer both those questions.

My Life In 10 Years

_____
_____
_____
_____
_____
_____
_____
_____
_____
_____
_____
_____
_____
_____
_____
_____
_____
_____
_____
_____
_____
_____
_____
_____
_____
_____
_____
_____
_____
_____

Workbook Companion for Girl Stop Apologizing by Rachel Hollis   BJ Richards

Next you need to take those 10 years and begin to organize it, narrow it down into bites. You're going to turn your ten years into ten dreams. Again, you need to be specific here and give yourself details to grasp onto.

1. Write those 10 dreams down here in detail. Maybe one of your is, "I only buy designer jeans," because that makes you feel beautiful and successful just thinking about it. The key is to phrase it in present tense, not future tense. After you write down the dream, write down why it's one of the steps that will get you closer. How will it make you feel? What will accomplishing just that one thing do for you inside? The more detail the better.

You can use the space I've provided for you here.

You'll also want to get yourself a notebook or a journal and write those 10 dreams down again and again every single day. Keep focusing on and repeating that every day so it's burned into your brain and your mind starts to draw it in.

(In case you missed it, I've created a journal specifically for you to use for your daily follow-up. *Journal for Girl Stop Apologizing by Rachel Hollis: A Shame-Free Plan for Embracing and Achieving Your Goals* by BJ Richards. You can learn more here: https://www.amazon.com/dp/109548060X)

64 | P a g e
Workbook Companion for Girl Stop Apologizing by Rachel Hollis
BJ Richards

Your 10 Dreams

_____
_____
_____
_____
_____
_____
_____
_____
_____
_____
_____
_____
_____
_____
_____
_____
_____
_____
_____
_____
_____
_____
_____
_____
_____
_____
_____
_____
_____

Workbook Companion for Girl Stop Apologizing by Rachel Hollis   BJ Richards

The last step in Ms. Hollis' 10/10/l exercise is to ask yourself what you can do right now. One thing out of the ten you just listed that you can start today that will get you closer to your 10-year goal.

1. Write that down here and be very specific. Have a clear picture of it in your head. What are the details, how will you gauge your progress along the way.
2. What is the emotional component behind the step you just wrote down? What do you feel when you think about reaching your goal? This is super important. Feeling yourself there and knowing you're doing the little things that lead to the finish line will keep you going because you can see it happening one step at a time. So take some time and list all the things you feel.

Behavior 3: Embrace Your Ambition

Key Points:

1. Ambition is a healthy tool.
2. Ambition comes with commitment and hard work.
3. Don't let other people's opinions deter your ambition.

Summary / Analysis:

The term "ambition" has had a bad rap in the past. But in reality, it is defined as a strong desire to achieve something. You need that to accomplish your goal. When you have ambition you have the determination to work hard toward your goal.

Your ambition is your drive. It's that energy that pushes you forward past the bumps in the road. Ambition properly channeled is a good thing, not a bad one. Yes, it can get out of control. But that's not what we're talking about it. We're talking about keeping the drive, the fortitude to keep after that goal until you get there.

Ambition is doing all the little things in your daily routine that keep you focused. Like getting up early to study or doing a work-out after the kids go to bed instead of sitting down in front of the TV.

It's the thing that makes you want to learn one more new thing, conquer one more chapter before you turn in, run just one more lap before you go home.

There may be thoughts running through your head like, "what if I get obsessive?" Worrying about a bunch of made-up scenarios that haven't even happened and likely won't happen is a huge waste of your time and energy. Don't go there. Use that focus to get your closer to your end point.

Or, "what will people think when they see me out there doing all this?" We already talked about that, remember? Who cares what they think? They're going to talk no matter what you do, so you might as well accomplish your dreams.

Actually achieving a goal can be scary, yes, because you've never done it before. You're going to be doing things that are different for you and some of them will be challenging. But that's okay. Everyone get nervous when they do something for the first time.

But that's what achievement is. Pushing through the butterflies in your stomach and accomplishing what you never thought you could.

You can do this if you choose to do it. Own your ambition. It's going to carry you through.

1. What are the extra steps your ambition will help you to get through on your journey? The details that are going the extra mile toward your goal. Is it getting up early, staying up late, taking a class?

_____
_____
_____
_____
_____
_____

2. What are the things that make you nervous about stepping out and into your power? The things that get the butterflies going in the pit of your stomach?

_____
_____
_____
_____
_____
_____

3. Is the idea of owning your ambition affecting your self-worth and confidence in any way? What is that and how does it make you feel?

_____
_____
_____
_____
_____
_____
_____

Workbook Companion for Girl Stop Apologizing by Rachel Hollis

BJ Richards

Behavior 4: Ask for Help!

Key Points:

1. Don't try to be super-woman.
2. Learn to delegate.
3. You're not doing this alone.

Summary / Analysis:

You're not super-woman. Nor are you supposed to be. You're going to need some help along the way if you want to get to your goal. That doesn't mean you're cheating. It means you're delegating some responsibilities so you can become the person you want to be.

Maybe one of your goals is to be on a champion bowling team. You have two small ones at home and the league meets on Thursday nights. You're going to need a baby-sitter. You can't drag them along to the bowling alley when they need to be in bed.

Face it, there comes a time along the way when you're going to ask for help. And you need to if you're going to get to that ten-year goal of who you want to be. If you try to do it all alone every step of the way you're going to burn out. And there goes your dream.

Maybe you'll need to hire someone to help with cleaning the house, or running errands. You can even work out trade arrangements if money is an issue.

Maybe you already have clients and you want to get to the next level. You may need to ask your existing clients to help put out the word about a new promotion or special you have coming up.

Asking for help is about being in the right frame of mind. It's about not being afraid to reach out for assistance to keep you on your journey. Yes, you're going to have some struggles. That doesn't mean your incapable and weak. It means you're a human being not a robot. Get help when you need it or you're going to burn out.

1. Is it hard for you to ask for help? Why do you think that is?

_____

_____

_____

_____

_____

_____

2. What are the things you can delegate to someone else to give you the time you need to accomplish your goal?

_____

_____

_____

_____

_____

_____

3. Who can you ask for help? A partner, friends, family?

_____

_____

_____

_____

_____

_____

_____

Workbook Companion for Girl Stop Apologizing by Rachel Hollis

BJ Richards

Behavior 5: Build Foundations for Success

Key Points:

1. You have to stay hydrated.
2. Get up an hour early.
3. Stop eating one kind of junk food for a month.
4. Get at least 30 minutes of exercise every day.
5. Keep a gratitude journal.

Summary / Analysis:

We've all heard the old saying that a house built on sand will eventually come tumbling down. Well, the same is true for us. If we don't have a firm foundation under us, we're setting ourselves up for disaster.

So specifically, what does that mean? It means taking care of yourself and not running yourself into the ground taking care of everyone else. If you go down, what good are you?

Ms. Hollis shares with us her "Five to Thrive". Those things she feels kept her strong enough to accomplish what she wanted to in her personal growth.

Number one on her list is hydration.

Are you healthy, truly healthy? Or are you just barely getting through the day. Do you drink enough water? Without proper hydration it's hard to lose weight and your body doesn't move the toxins through your system efficiently. That can make you feel run down and sluggish. Ms. Hollis recommends drinking half your weight in water. And yes, it means you'll be running to the bathroom. That's good because it's flushing the toxins so your body works better and you last longer.

Number Two of Ms. Hollis' "Five to Thrive" is get up an hour early.

Get up before the rest of the family so you have some time to yourself. Now for some of you this isn't going to work because you're up half the night with an infant anyway or your job has you up before dawn as it is. Then come up with another option for yourself.

Number three of Ms. Hollis' Five-to-Thrive is staying away from one category of junk food for a month.

We're not talking about the good food you should be eating like fruits and vegetables. We're talking about cookies, or chips or the ice cream you keep in the freezer. You're creating another good habit here. You're teaching yourself to keep a promise to yourself for a month.

One continuous 30 days. Not 10 days of doing it and then 2 days of "oops". Because if you do that you have to start over again. You're proving to yourself that you've got what it takes to persevere. You'll be so proud of yourself when you accomplish this you won't believe it.

Number four of Ms. Hollis' Five-to-Thrive: Move your body every day.

Exercise at least 30 minutes every day. It's a fact that the most successful people on the planet work out at least 5 days out of 7. Spend energy and get energy. That's the way it works. And you need energy to accomplish your goal.

The fifth thing in Ms. Hollis' Five-to-thrive is: Practice gratitude daily.

You'll find this inspiring and fun. You're going to list ten things every day you're grateful for. Make this list about things that happened today; about what's going on right now.

The idea here is to start looking for those everyday things that are a blessing to you. This little exercise helps to change your perspective on life from negative to positive. You'll start to see sunshine in your day where before you didn't even notice it. And you'll start to feel happier and more alive.

Out of the five steps in Ms. Hollis' Five-To-thrive, she states this is the most important one. Even if you feel you can't do all the others, at least do this one. And do it consistently for 30 days so it becomes a habit. This is setting yourself up for success. This is helping you keep your vision strong.

You'll want to get a separate notebook or journal for this eventually. But you can start right now using the space here.

(**In case you missed it, I've developed a journal specifically for you to address this**: *Journal for Girl Stop Apologizing by Rachel Hollis: A Shame-Free Plan for Embracing and Achieving Your Goals* by BJ Richards. It's the perfect companion to this workbook and Ms. Hollis' original work. You can learn more here: https://www.amazon.com/dp/109548060X)

Next is getting your personal space in order. Is it clean, neat, well organized? Are there reminders in your home about what you're working toward. Maybe put stickies on the mirror and on the kitchen cupboard. Or put photos you've cut out of a magazine of how you envision yourself in 10 years.

You're building a foundation for your future, so you want it to be solid, firm and nice.

What about your community? We tend to be a reflection of the five people we're around the most. Why? Because we're hearing their words, perhaps sharing their points of view and imitating their habits.

If you're the one everyone else is looking up to for inspiration and guidance, then you need to add other people to your life that you can draw inspiration from. You need to have people around you who represent qualities you can emulate and aspire to.

As you pursue your dream you must be consistent. Consistency is the key to everything. We didn't learn to write our names in one day. We practiced over and over until we were able to do it without thinking. Consistency makes habits. And you're trying to set yourself up with fantastic habits that will make yourself successful.

So how do you recognize your habits? First understand that habits consist of 3 things:

1. A cue. A trigger. A signal to your brain that it's time to take action.
2. An action. Now that your brain has the signal, you automatically do something without thinking.
3. A reward. Something happens that you want.

This can be a life affirming process or end up a debilitating one. If you constantly overeat (the action) to get through the stress (the trigger), you'll feel momentarily satisfied (the reward). But then you start berating yourself for overeating and feeling like a complete loser. So you start the cycle all over again.

Start paying attention to what you do and what sets you off. This is important information that can help you turn things around.

Next is your morning routine. Do you have one? If your morning starts out chaotic, you'll carry that over with you when you get to work or

Workbook Companion for Girl Stop Apologizing by Rachel Hollis

however you spend your day. You'll already be in a harried mindset and it will much more difficult to do what needs to be done because of it.

This is the morning routine Ms. Hollis has shared that works for her. This will give you an idea so you can develop your own.

1. She gets up at 5 am. Has a glass of water and a cup of coffee. Then goes to work on her big project for herself.
2. 15 minutes of gratitude meditation.
3. Writes in her journal about her intentions for the day, things she's grateful for and an affirmation of who she wants to be.
4. Wakes up the kids.
5. After the kids are at school, she gets ready to upbeat music.
6. Once ready for work she makes a green smoothie.
7. Then she writes down her list of 10 dreams and the one goal that's going to get her there the fastest.

1. What is your one junk food that you're going to give up for 30 days? Why did you choose that one?

_____
_____
_____
_____
_____
_____

2. What exercise are you going to do every day for at least 30 minutes? Run, walk, workout?

_____
_____
_____
_____
_____
_____

3. What are 10 things you're grateful for that have taken place in the last 24 hours.

_____
_____
_____
_____
_____
_____

Workbook Companion for Girl Stop Apologizing by Rachel Hollis

4. Write out 3 things you can do to make your personal space a true foundation that reflects your goal and makes a statement about who you believe you are becoming.

_____

_____

_____

_____

_____

_____

5. Who are the five people you're around the most? Is there one person in that group who has qualities you'd like to emulate? Where do you stand in that group? Do you feel you need to expand it?

_____

_____

_____

_____

_____

_____

6. Take a look at your habits. Make a list of the life-affirming habits you have that are going to help you accomplish your goal. What are the habits you would like to change?

_____

_____

_____

_____

_____

_____

_____

What is your morning routine? Write it out here. If you don't have one, sketch it out.

_____
_____
_____
_____
_____
_____
_____
_____
_____
_____
_____
_____
_____
_____
_____
_____
_____
_____
_____
_____
_____
_____
_____
_____
_____
_____
_____
_____

Behavior 6: Stop Allowing Them to Talk You Out of It

Key Points:

1. People in your life may start to feel left out.
2. Evaluate the people around you and the impact they're having on you.
3. Be prepared to handle non-supportive friends or family.
4. Plan and schedule ahead to make things run smoother.

Summary / Analysis:

Let's talk about our friends and family. Yes, the love us and they want the best for us. But the time may come when they start to feel left out. Your "spare" time is going in another direction toward your goal and not to them and they're going to feel it.

We've all been at the end of the "just this once" scenario. Maybe it's a birthday and everyone has to have a piece of the cake; and not partaking looks like you're not celebrating. Or you need to go for your run and your friend desperately wants you to just forget it for today because she wants to talk over coffee.

Workbook Companion for Girl Stop Apologizing by Rachel Hollis

You're going to run into this in different ways, so you need to be prepared.

Stop and evaluate the people you have in your life.

1. Is there someone around you now who isn't supporting your choice to improve yourself?
2. Is this person outwardly not supporting you by being negative, mean, making you feel guilty or anxious?
3. What is the price you're paying by keeping that person in your life? Diminished self-esteem, headaches every time you encounter them?
4. Do you really want to continue seeing that person?

The next step is to be prepared before you go to see them again. The solution isn't always to cut them out of your life, but to recognize what they're doing to you because of their own insecurities and issues. Figure out ahead of time how you're going to react and what you're going to say to circumvent their negativity.

1. What is likely to come up when you see that person?
2. What responses can you have ready to go when they make their comments?
3. If it's an event where there will be a lot of food you don't want to eat, can you eat before you go so you're not as hungry? Or can you suggest a different restaurant where there's food you can eat if that's the problem?

And finally, what can you do to plan and schedule things ahead of time to make it easier for all concerned? Your new goal and plan is going to have an impact on others around you. What steps can you pre-plan to make it easier for everyone? Can you cook meals ahead, line up a sitter if needed?

1. If this area is one that you're going to deal with list what you can do to help others deal with the change.

2. What are you going to say to help them understand how important this is to you?

1. Who are the people in your life your new lifestyle will have the most impact on? Is there anyone who is outwardly negative or non-supportive? How does that affect you completing your goal?

_____
_____
_____
_____
_____
_____

2. How can you plan ahead to make your new schedule comfortable for everyone? Get a sitter, pre-cook meals?

_____
_____
_____
_____
_____
_____

3. How are you going to explain your new schedule and goal to those people that are important to you?

_____
_____
_____
_____
_____
_____
_____

Workbook Companion for Girl Stop Apologizing by Rachel Hollis

Behavior 7: Learn to Say No

Key Points:

1. Know what your priorities are and keep them firmly implanted in your mind.
2. If an invitation doesn't feel like a "hell, yes!", then it's a "no".
3. Don't let invitations sit. Respond ASAP.
4. Be honest and polite when turning down an invitation.
5. Be firm if you don't want to accept; don't leave an invitation open-ended.

Summary / Analysis:

You've established your schedule now and there are going to be people you'll want you to abandon your goal for their events. You don't have to explain what's going on in your life to everyone. But you are going to have to learn to say no to keep your commitment to yourself.

Here are Ms. Hollis' 3 rules for saying no to invitations she doesn't want to accept. Remember, every hour you commit to a function or a gathering is an hour you're taking away from your goal or your family time.

Rule #1:

Workbook Companion for Girl Stop Apologizing by Rachel Hollis

Respond ASAP. Don't beat around the bush and wait until the last minute when you can't cancel. You'll end up at a function you don't want to be at and that can turn into a bad attitude about the whole event. This isn't helping anyone.

Rule #2:

Be polite but honest. If the commitments are taking time away from your family, say so. No one is going to argue with that.

Rule #3:

Be firm. If you're not firm, then people will come back repeatedly to ask you for the same thing over and over in an effort to wear you down. You also have to be firm with yourself. Keep your goal in mind and stick to it. Don't rob yourself of your future.

1. How do you say no when asked to do something you'd rather not?

_____
_____
_____
_____
_____
_____

2. Do you feel good about how you handled it? If not, what can you change in your approach?

_____
_____
_____
_____
_____
_____

3. Do you let people talk you into events you'd rather not be at? How do you feel when that happens?

_____
_____
_____
_____
_____
_____

Workbook Companion for Girl Stop Apologizing by Rachel Hollis

BJ Richards

Part III: Skills to Acquire

First let's talk about the difference between a skill and a talent. A skill is something you can learn by training with someone through a class or life experience. Maybe you learned to sew from your mother or in a Home Economics class in high school. A talent is a trait you have a natural aptitude for that you were born with. Perhaps you have a natural singing voice or you're just naturally great with math.

We're going to be talking about skills. Something you can practice and use until you become an expert at it. So don't worry if you don't feel accomplished about the things being covered in this part. You can practice and learn as you go.

Skill 1: Planning

Key Points:

1. To achieve your goal you must know where you're going.
2. Your plan must have a starting point and an end point.
3. You need sign-posts along the way so you know you're on track.
4. Go all in.

Summary / Analysis:

You need to know where you're going. That means you need two specific pieces of information: Where you are right now, and where you want to end up.

After that you need to have sign posts along the way so you know you're not lost and still on track. Not having a plan in place, something tangible that you can look at and touch and understand, is one of the main reasons you may have failed getting to where you wanted to go in life.

Start with where you want to end up and go backwards. It will help you figure out the steps you need in-between. It's going to take some honest soul-searching to get there.

Take your time to write out answers to the following questions. You'll use these answers to plot out your plan. Say for example you're a stay-

Workbook Companion for Girl Stop Apologizing by Rachel Hollis

at-home-mom with a goal to lose 20 pounds. Now you know where you want to go.

Maybe one of your current assets is a sister who is already dieting and you can use her as a support for when you are dying to eat that chocolate cake. A trait that's working against you might be over eating. You could develop a new habit of drinking extra water and hot tea throughout the day to keep you feeling full and less hungry. You get the idea.

1. List the assets you currently have that will help you attain your goal. Resources, habits, anything you have right now that you can put to immediate use.

_____

_____

_____

_____

_____

_____

2. List the traits and habits you have that may work against you.

_____

_____

_____

_____

_____

_____

3. For each item listed in number 2 (things that could work against you), describe a new habit or trait you could develop to take its place.

_____

_____

_____

_____

_____

_____

_____

Workbook Companion for Girl Stop Apologizing by Rachel Hollis   BJ Richards

Now you're going to do something called mind mapping. Don't get confused about the term. It's the same thing as brainstorming. On the page that's included here start writing down everything that comes into your head you may need to do along the way to get to your goal.

Let's use the weight loss example. You might have things like cleaning the junk food out of the cupboard, buying a food scale, posting photos of the dress you want to get into around the house, etc. Write, scribble, draw circles, arrows pointing from one thing to another because they're related, etc.

Remember, this is writing down everything that just pops into your head. You can analyze and delete later. You can use the form on the next page (Brainstorm Mind Map #1), or you can just use a piece of blank paper. I think you'll find this part fun!

Brainstorming Mind Map #1

You know your finish line, your goal. Use the circles and the space around them to come up with as many ideas as possible to get you there. What will you need to know, who will you need to hire, what will you need to do. Try to come up with at least 20 ideas.

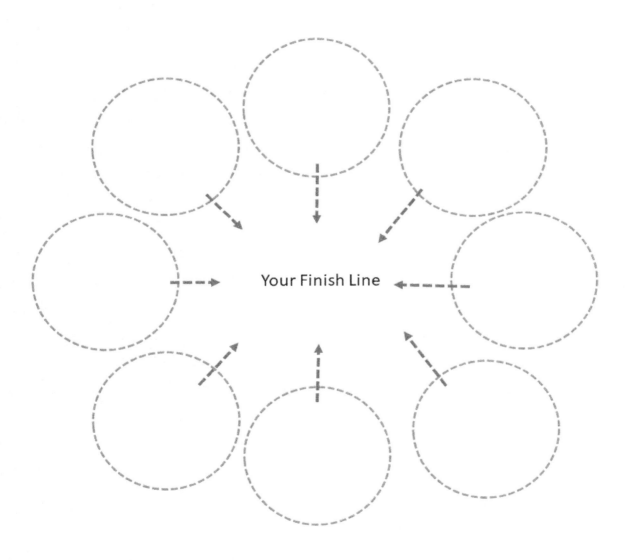

Your Finish Line

Workbook Companion for Girl Stop Apologizing by Rachel Hollis

Now that you have this wonderful collage of stuff all over your paper you're going to start to analyze it. Get out a colored pen or a highlighter. Think of your end goal where you want to end up. Now look at your mind map/brainstorming and find the one thing that you need to have in place right before you reach that end point; the step you need to accomplish right before you complete your goal. Write GP#3 beside it.

Now find the one that comes before that. Label it GP#2.

And one more that comes before that. Mark that one GP#1.

Highlight those. These are your guideposts, the things that will help to keep you on your journey. And the things you can use to get you back on track if you stray. Don't get all caught up in the "how" right now. You'll drive yourself crazy and stop before you even start, so don't go there. Right now all we're doing is working on the steps.

You should be very proud of yourself. You've just established a starting point, an end point, and three guideposts to keep you on track. Hurray!

Next Part:

Okay, now we're ready for the "how". These are the smaller steps in-between. If you were on a road they would be mile markers and there are lots of those. You're going to use the same exercise you did before and do another mind-mapping/brainstorming session. But this time you're going to look at your starting point, where you are right now.

In the next form I've provided (Brainstorm Mind Map #2), you're going to brainstorm the answer to this question: What actions and resources do I need to do to get from the beginning of my goal to my first guidepost (GP#1)?

Remember this is a free-flowing exercise. Don't think, just write down all the things that come into your head on the sheet here. If you need extra sheets, grab a notebook and keep going. This is a list of possibles, not "yes" you're going to do them all. You're writing as fast as you can and everything that comes into your head. If we use our weight loss example, you might be listing things like joining a weight loss group, finding an exercise buddy, etc.

Brainstorm MindMap#2

Now that you know your starting point, you need to know the steps from there to your first Guide Post. Use the circles and the space around them to come up with as many ideas as you can to get you from the start to Guide Post #1.

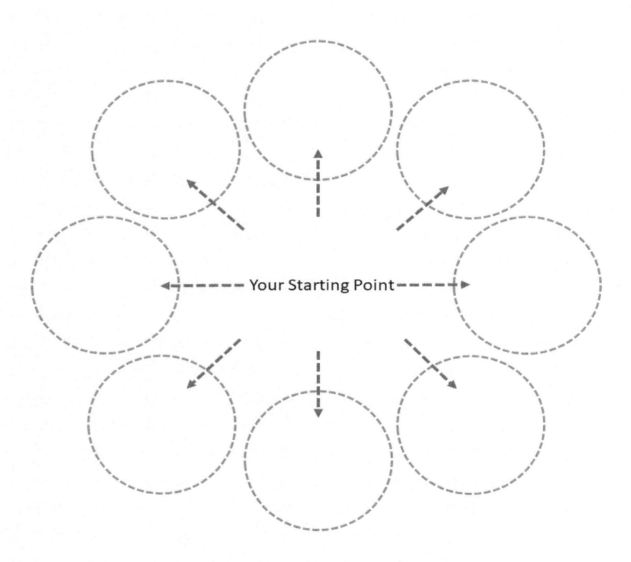

Your Starting Point

Now you're going to divide those up into three lists: Daily, Weekly, Monthly. Those are your steps that are telling you the "how". That will get you from your starting point to your achievement. These are the mile markers.

I've provided a page divided into those three columns (Mile Markers: Start to Guidepost #1). If you need more space, you can use an additional sheet of notepaper.

Mile Markers: Start to Guide Post #1

Daily	Weekly	Monthly
_____	_____	_____
_____	_____	_____
_____	_____	_____
_____	_____	_____
_____	_____	_____
_____	_____	_____
_____	_____	_____
_____	_____	_____
_____	_____	_____
_____	_____	_____
_____	_____	_____
_____	_____	_____
_____	_____	_____
_____	_____	_____
_____	_____	_____

You'll follow the same process for getting from Guidepost #1 to Guidepost #2. And for getting from Guidepost #2 to Guidepost #3. Then from Guidepost #3 to the finish line.

First, you'll do a brainstorm/mind map. Then you'll divide those ideas into the three columns.

So next, do the brainstorming/mind mapping for getting from Guidepost #1 to Guidepost #2. List everything you can think of that will help you get there on the sheet I've provided for you here (Brainstorm Mind Map #3). Try to come up with at least 20 ideas.

Workbook Companion for Girl Stop Apologizing by Rachel Hollis

Brainstorm MindMap#3

Brain storm from Guide Post #1 to Guide Post #2. Write down everything you can think of to get you there. Use the circles and the space around them to come up with as many ideas as you can.

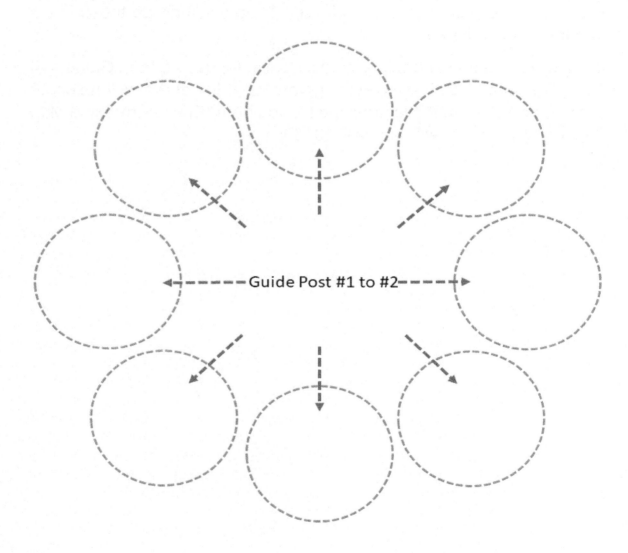

Guide Post #1 to #2

Workbook Companion for Girl Stop Apologizing by Rachel Hollis

Now you're going to divide those up into three lists: Daily, Weekly, Monthly. Those are your steps telling you the "how". Those are your mile markers. They tell you how you're going to get from Guidepost #1 to Guidepost #2.

I've provided a page for you divided into those three columns (Mile Markers: Guide Post #1 to GP#2). If you need additional space, you can use a sheet of notepaper.

Mile Markers: Guide Post #1 to GP#2

Daily	Weekly	Monthly
_____	_____	_____
_____	_____	_____
_____	_____	_____
_____	_____	_____
_____	_____	_____
_____	_____	_____
_____	_____	_____
_____	_____	_____
_____	_____	_____
_____	_____	_____
_____	_____	_____
_____	_____	_____
_____	_____	_____
_____	_____	_____
_____	_____	_____
_____	_____	_____

Workbook Companion for Girl Stop Apologizing by Rachel Hollis

You'll follow the same process for getting from Guidepost #2 to Guidepost #3.

Do a brainstorm/mind map for getting from Guidepost #2 to Guidepost #3. List everything you can think of that will help you get there on the sheet I've provided for you here (Brainstorm Mind Map #4). Try to come up with at least 20 ideas.

Brainstorm MindMap#4

Brain storm from Guide Post #2 to Guide Post #3. Write down everything you can think of to get you there. Use the circles and the space around them to come up with as many ideas as you can.

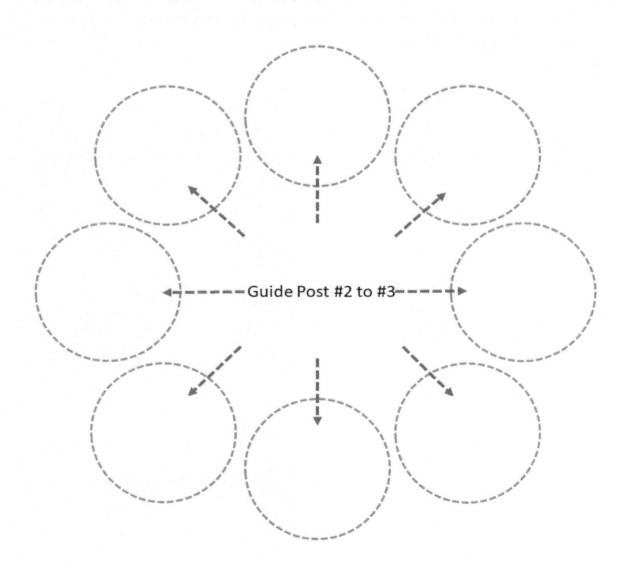

Guide Post #2 to #3

Workbook Companion for Girl Stop Apologizing by Rachel Hollis

Now you're going to divide those up into three lists: Daily, Weekly, Monthly. Those are your steps telling you the "how". Those are your mile markers. They tell you how you're going to get from Guidepost #2 to Guidepost #3.

I've provided a page for you divided into those three columns (Mile Markers: Guidepost #2 to GP#3). If you need additional space, you can use a sheet of notepaper.

Mile Markers: Guidepost #2 to GP#3

Daily	Weekly	Monthly
_____	_____	_____
_____	_____	_____
_____	_____	_____
_____	_____	_____
_____	_____	_____
_____	_____	_____
_____	_____	_____
_____	_____	_____
_____	_____	_____
_____	_____	_____
_____	_____	_____
_____	_____	_____
_____	_____	_____
_____	_____	_____
_____	_____	_____
_____	_____	_____
_____	_____	_____

Workbook Companion for Girl Stop Apologizing by Rachel Hollis

Keep going… you're almost there!

Now for the last brainstorming/mind mapping session. You're going to do exactly as before, but this time you're brainstorming getting from Guidepost #3 to the Finish Line. Hooray!

Try to come up with at least 20 ideas. I've provided a form for you to use (Brainstorm Mind Map#5). If you'd prefer to use a blank piece of paper, that's fine, too.

Brainstorm MindMap#5

Brain storm from Guide Post #3 to your finish line. Write down everything you can think of to get you there. Use the circles and the space around them to come up with as many ideas as you can.

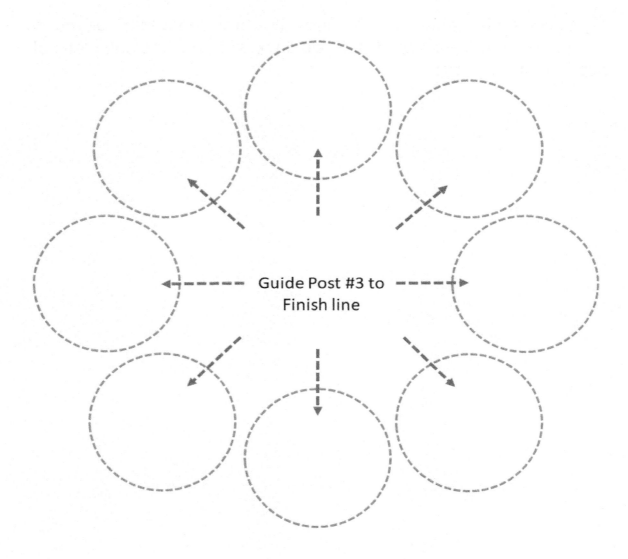

Guide Post #3 to
Finish line

Now you're going to divide those up into three lists: Daily, Weekly, Monthly. Those are your steps telling you the "how". Those are your mile markers. They tell you how you're going to get from Guidepost #3 to the Finish Line.

I've provided a page for you divided into those three columns (Mile Markers: Guide Post #3 to Finish). If you need additional space, you can use a sheet of notepaper.

Workbook Companion for Girl Stop Apologizing by Rachel Hollis

Mile Markers: Guide Post #3 to Finish

Daily	Weekly	Monthly
_____	_____	_____
_____	_____	_____
_____	_____	_____
_____	_____	_____
_____	_____	_____
_____	_____	_____
_____	_____	_____
_____	_____	_____
_____	_____	_____
_____	_____	_____
_____	_____	_____
_____	_____	_____
_____	_____	_____
_____	_____	_____
_____	_____	_____
_____	_____	_____

On Your Road Map below, you're going to write in your start, finish and three guideposts. This is your road map. Then you'll refer to the lists you've just made for the mile markers in-between.

Great job! This is a process and you've accomplished a big thing just in doing your roadmap. You should be very proud of yourself.

Your Road Map

1 Your Starting Point

2 Guide Post #1

3 Guide Post #2

4 Guide Post #3

5 Your Finish Line!

Last step: Go All In. Three little words you're going to use for the encouragement you need to get you through the tough times when you may want to throw in the towel. Stickies are perfect for this. Or a personalized screen saver on your phone or computer. Put them up everywhere. You'll be amazed at how effective it is.

Skill 2: Confidence

Key Points:

1. You can learn to be confident.
2. When you look good, you feel good.
3. Do you best with what you know.
4. Who you hang out with matters.

Summary / Analysis:

Dictionary.com defines confidence as: "belief in one's self and one's powers or abilities".

It means you can count on yourself to come through. And it's another skill you can learn and get great at. How do you do that? By working on three key things: your appearance, your actions and who you hang out with.

We'll start with Part 1: Your Appearance

Let's face it, when we look good, we feel better about ourselves. If you're having a great hair day you know it and it shows. If you just put on a new dress you've been eyeing forever you feel like a million bucks. You have to like the way you look. You're an individual with your own personal style and you'll want to express that in a positive way.

BJ Richards
Workbook Companion for Girl Stop Apologizing by Rachel Hollis

Part 2: Your Actions

This one is a little tougher. Sometimes you have to pretend to be confident when you're really not. You have to put yourself out there and try even though you haven't done something before. That doesn't mean you can't connect the dots and do it based on what experience you already have. There's a first time for anything. And to give ourselves the chance to get to that first time, we have to jump in and do our best based on what we already know. We have to give ourselves a little push.

Part 3: Who you hang out with matters.

It's a fact. Other people influence us, through their actions and their words. The more you're around confident people, the more confident you will become. You'll just automatically begin to emulate their habits and patterns.

Pay attention to what makes you feel confident, where you are and who you're with. Find ways to give yourself more of those opportunities.

1. How do you feel about the way you look? Is there anything you'd like to change? Can you think of anything that would specifically make you feel more confident?

_____
_____
_____
_____
_____
_____

2. Was there ever a time in your life when you had to pretend you were confident when you really didn't feel like you knew what you were doing? What was that? How did you do?

_____
_____
_____
_____
_____
_____

3. How many of your friends are in the confidence league you'd like to see yourself in? Are those people in your top five we talked about earlier? If needed, what can you do to change that and how?

_____
_____
_____
_____
_____
_____
_____

Workbook Companion for Girl Stop Apologizing by Rachel Hollis
BJ Richards

Skill 3: Persistence

Key Points:

1. You're in this for the long haul.
2. Don't put a deadline on your goal.
3. Don't think small.
4. Read about others who've achieved their dreams for inspiration.

Summary / Analysis:

The first thing to do here is forget the timeline. Your journey may be super- fast, and because you've done such a great job with your planning and following your heart, you'll reach your goal before you know it. But, more times than not, things take longer than we thought. And if you miss that deadline it will make you want to give up.

So don't put yourself in that position.

Remember, you're in this for the long haul. If your dream was easy, you'd already have done it. So expand your perspective, and stop thinking small. Time is going to pass no matter what you're doing with it. You can spend an hour sitting on the couch watching TV or you can spend that hour exercising and getting healthier. It's the same amount of time either way and it's going to go by regardless of what you're doing. So you might as well spend it achieving your goal and living your dreams.

Sometimes it's helpful to remind ourselves of others who made it happen and didn't give up on themselves. Walt Disney, Madonna, Oprah... all hit major stumbling blocks at different points in their lives. But they persevered, and look what they accomplished.

You can do it, too.

1. Is there anything you're thinking small about right now that will affect your goal? What would be a better perspective?

_____
_____
_____
_____
_____
_____

2. List three people you've heard about who didn't give up on their dreams that you can draw inspiration from.

_____
_____
_____
_____
_____
_____

3. What is one characteristic each of those people have you can use as a role model for yourself?

_____
_____
_____
_____
_____
_____
_____

Skill 4: Effectiveness

Key Points:

1. Find a place to work where you won't be distracted.
2. Turn off all digital devices so you can keep your focus.
3. Turn your to-do list into a results list.
4. Know what distracts you and avoid those things.
5. Re-Evaluate your plan on a weekly basis.

Summary / Analysis:

Find a place to work at your goal where you won't be distracted. If you're trying to work out and the family keeps interrupting asking for something, it's taking twice as long to accomplish your workout. Consider going to a gym or some other place where that won't happen.

Same thing with digital devices. If you're trying to write or study, turn off the phone and close down all your social media sites so you're not paying more attention to them than accomplishing your goal. You've carved out your sacred hours and you need to honor yourself and your commitment to your goal. Scrolling Instagram or Facebook isn't getting you any closer to your goal and you're losing valuable time.

The ability to focus is key to accomplishing anything. The following five rules will help you stay productive and get you where you're going.

Number one: Make A Results List Instead Of A To-Do List

A to-do list can keep you stuck in the same spot if you're not careful. It can cause you to continuously widen the point you're already at instead of moving on to the next point when you really could. That's because there are usually twenty plus items on that list that don't really relate to what you need to get done during the goal session for just today.

A Results List is different because it's going to focus on what you need to accomplish from that one session. If you're trying to lose weight, you might have things like: Worked out for 30 minutes, threw all the junk food out of the cupboards, drank hot tea instead of grabbing one more thing to eat.

Your Results List isn't going to be any more than 5 items. It may only be 2 or 3 items. But they will be important things that push you along. Keep it short and doable for this one session. If you don't, you're going to overwhelm yourself and end up frustrated. So make the things on that list doable and steps that push you forward. You'll have a feeling of wild accomplishment this way. Why? Because you can see your goal is getting closer and closer and is really happening.

That is your new habit. That feeling of accomplishment and moving forward. So do the Results List instead of the To-Do List.

Number Two: Take a fresh look at how you're doing things.

Gary Keller asks a great question in his book *The One Thing*. One that you should ask every day when you look at your results list. Ask yourself what the one thing is you can do today that would make everything else on the list simpler, better, faster.

If you were trying to write a book or study for a test, you might need to go to the library and plug-in there away from people who might interrupt you during your session.

Workbook Companion for Girl Stop Apologizing by Rachel Hollis

Number Three: You Need A Productive Environment

It's important you know what helps you to concentrate, no matter where you are. There isn't always going to be the perfect office to work in or the ultimate gym to train in. But that doesn't mean you still can't accomplish your session for the day and get closer to your goal.

That's where your zone triggers come in. Those things that help you focus and get productive. For some people, it's listening to a certain type of music that gets the buzz going. Or having a latte or iced tea within arm's reach. For others it may be snack food they munch on or a particular gum they like to chew.

It doesn't really matter what it is. But it does matter that you can identify what it is for you. That way you can purposely set yourself up for a productive session even if it's writing in the car while you wait for the kids to finish their after-school activities.

Number Four: Avoid Known Distractions

Start paying attention to the things that pull your attention away when you're trying to concentrate. Is it text notifications on your phone, or an open tab to Facebook or social media? Maybe something you were wondering about pops into your head so you stop to look it up before you forget again.

All those distractions add up and take you away from your accomplishment. They draw you further from your goal instead of pushing you closer to it.

So turn the sound off your phone, close down the extra tabs if you need to be on the computer to work and turn off the wi-fi if necessary.

Number Five: Re-Evaluate Your Course On a Weekly Basis

Now you're going to sit back and evaluate what has happened for the last week. Did you get where you wanted to go? Are the steps you've

Workbook Companion for Girl Stop Apologizing by Rachel Hollis

BJ Richards

been taking pushing you toward the next mile marker? Are you really heading in the right direction, or have you veered off the road?

If everything you've been doing is right on track, then woo-hoo!

If not, then it's time for a course correction. What can you do to get things back on track? Look at everything you had scheduled for the upcoming week and re-evaluate it. Ask yourself if what you had planned is specific and pushing you forward in the right direction.

Do this every week and try to do it on the same day. Pick a day when you're setting up your plans for the coming week, like a Sunday.

1. What are your zone triggers? The things you do that help you to concentrate and focus. A favorite song, a cup of coffee? What helps you to concentrate regardless of where you are?

_____

_____

_____

_____

_____

_____

2. What are your known distractions? What can you do to avoid them?

_____

_____

_____

_____

_____

_____

3. Is there one thing you can do to accomplish your goal faster or easier? What is that? What is the best day to do your weekly evaluation?

_____

_____

_____

_____

_____

_____

_____

Skill 5: Positivity

Key Points:

1. You can choose how to handle any situation.
2. Happiness is a choice.
3. Your attitude is everything.
4. Practice gratitude daily.
5. You have to monitor your self-talk.

Summary / Analysis

There is always going to be something going on that isn't perfect. The phone keeps ringing, the kids are fighting, you're out of the one thing you need to finish fixing dinner. The only thing that's going to keep you from going crazy is your attitude. How you handle it, your mindset.

You have to choose happiness and gratitude daily. You have to make it a habit to find the good in everyday life. And that means you have to monitor what you say to yourself… the thoughts in your head.

Everything you say to yourself has an impact. All those nagging little digs of not being good enough or being too fat or too stupid takes a toll. Your self-talk is playing in the background all day, every day and it's affecting your attitude about life.

You have to choose to change it.

It's going to be hard not to freak out when the kids have acted up for the 20th time, when all day you've been telling yourself you're not good enough and never will be. That kind of self-talk already has you depressed and ready to cry as it is.

Now is the time to turn your self-talk around. To consciously catch yourself every time you start saying negative things to yourself and focus on something positive instead. Yes, it's going to take some time to reprogram yourself, but it's completely doable.

You may be trying really hard to have a good day and instead everything goes wrong. Events will happen you can't control. But you can control and change how you react to them.

Start looking for the light at the end of the tunnel. You don't have to have every solution to every problem, but you can start to poke some holes into the problem and let some sunshine in. And you're going to do that with your attitude.

Start by practicing gratitude daily, in your head all day long. Let gratitude replace the negative self-talk. Instead of telling yourself you're too fat, focus on how nice it is to be home in a clean house.

The more you do this, the better your attitude will become. You'll start feeling better about yourself and life will be happier and easier.

1. What is your usual go-to attitude when things go wrong? Would you like to change that? What would you like it to be?

_____
_____
_____
_____
_____
_____

2. What does your self-talk sound like? Is there anything about that you'd like to change? If so, what is it?

_____
_____
_____
_____
_____
_____

3. Do you practice gratitude daily? What are 3 things you're grateful for that have happened today.

_____
_____
_____
_____
_____
_____
_____

Workbook Companion for Girl Stop Apologizing by Rachel Hollis

Skill 6: Lead-Her-Ship

Key Points:

1. Embrace your leadership.
2. Every woman deserves the chance to be her greatest potential.
3. By pursuing your own goal, you're inspiring the world around you.

Summary / Analysis:

Believe it or not, you're a leader. You don't have to run a company or be in charge of the local women's group to be a leader. A leader is someone who is living their truth and doing it with purpose and direction. Someone who cares about themselves and wants to have a positive impact on their world.

Are you a teacher? Then let the kids see how they can help others by watching you. Are you an administrative assistant? Then inspire everyone in the office by your motivation and attitude.

Love what you live. Everything you do and say can have an impact on someone. You may not know it at the time, but that doesn't mean it doesn't happen. That compliment you gave to the neighbor next door may have brightened her whole day and turned her depression around. And when she went to market, she passed it on the clerk because she was feeling so good about herself inside.

You're setting an example when your confidence glows around you like a beacon. Your confidence is inspiring someone else all the time. You're being a leader through your actions, your attitude, your mindset.

This is why pursuing your goal and your dream is so important. Yes, you're doing it for yourself. But people around you are getting in on the excitement too. They see you moving forward, and it gives them the push the need to do it, too. They see it's not hopeless and it can be done. That life can change and get better.

Hope is everything. Leaders offer hope through encouragement. They let their light shine on the path behind them so the next one doesn't trip on the rock they had to overcome. They share what they learn.

Let your magic out. Let your energy glow. You'll not only inspire yourself; you'll inspire your world.

1. Do you feel like you are a leader? Why or why not?

_____
_____
_____
_____
_____
_____

2. What qualities do you have that are leadership qualities? What can you do to further develop your leadership qualities?

_____
_____
_____
_____
_____
_____

3. How can you use your qualities to lead and inspire others?

_____
_____
_____
_____
_____
_____
_____

Workbook Companion for Girl Stop Apologizing by Rachel Hollis

Conclusion

Summary / Analysis:

It all boils down to you believing in yourself. Believing enough to give yourself a chance. Believing enough to take the steps, to do the road map, to pick yourself up after a crummy day.

You can read a hundred how-to books and watch a hundred inspiring movies. But if you don't take the action steps nothing is going to change. You have to show up. You have to be your own cheerleader. You have to dig in and do the work, because no one else is going to do it for you.

This is not a sprint. You're not barreling down the road full speed and then slamming on the brakes. This is the long haul. This is your life.

You're going to do it one day at a time. And if that puts you over the top, then do it one hour at time. But you can do it. You just have to keep reminding yourself: *This is me. This is who I am.*

Reflect back on the visualization you did. The one where you visualized who you wanted to become. That's you on the inside. It's that bigger, better, happier part you dreamed about. And it's who you can become if you choose it.

So stop apologizing for your dream and accept your own challenge. Give yourself a chance. And become who you are longing to be.

Thank you.

I want to thank you for purchasing this workbook. I hope you've enjoyed completing it as much as I've enjoyed writing it and it helps you on your path toward your goal and your dream.

You can stay in touch with me at my website:
https://bjrichardsauthor.com

Or on my Facebook page:
https://www.facebook.com/BJ.Richards.Author/

And be sure to check out the other books I've written. You can see some of them on the Recommended Reading pages I've included here, or at my website.

Good luck on your journey to a happier, healthier you!

Workbook Companion for Girl Stop Apologizing by Rachel Hollis

Recommended Reading

I'm sure you already have this, but if not, it's highly recommended you get a copy of the original work, as this workbook is a companion to it.

Girl, Stop Apologizing: A Shame-Free Plan for Embracing and Achieving Your Goals by Rachel Hollis

You can purchase it here: https://www.amazon.com/Girl-Stop-Apologizing-Shame-Free-Embracing-ebook/dp/B07DT7VJ8T

Recommended: Get The Whole Set

The Perfect Journal for This Program:

You're going to need a place to write out your daily steps as you go through the program like: The ten things you're grateful for each day, your intention for the day, tracking your daily habits, notes, etc.

No problem... I have it covered for you! **My journal is designed specifically for the program presented by Ms. Hollis** in her original work, *Girl Stop Apologizing*. This will help you make your journey even easier!

Journal for Girl Stop Apologizing by Rachel Hollis: A Shame-Free Plan for Embracing and Achieving Your Goals by BJ Richards.

The Perfect Planner for This Program:

A planner will be essential to your journey. You'll want a place to set up, track and change your schedule on a weekly, monthly and yearly basis.

I have that covered for you, too! **My planner is designed specifically for the program presented by Ms. Hollis** in her original work, *Girl Stop Apologizing*. This will help you make your journey even easier!

Planner for Girl Stop Apologizing by Rachel Hollis: A Shame-Free Plan for Embracing and Achieving Your Goals by BJ Richards

You may also be interested in some of my other books:

1) Find out what coconut oil can really do for you without all the hype. Check out my best-selling book: *Coconut Oil Breakthrough: Boost Your Brain, Burn the Fat, Build Your Hair* by BJ Richards

Check it out here: https://www.amazon.com/Coconut-Oil-Breakthrough-Boost-Brain-ebook/dp/B01EGBA1FW/

2) Do you have a dog? Here's another best seller you may be interested in. You'll find out to deal with a number of issues safely and inexpensively at home. Find out all about it in my best-seller: *Coconut Oil and My Dog: Natural Pet Health for My Canine Friend* by BJ Richards

You can check it out here: https://www.amazon.com/Coconut-Oil-My-Dog-Natural-ebook/dp/B01MUF93U1/

3) Did you know apple cider vinegar and baking soda have some amazing health benefits? Plus, you can use them for so many things in the home and save a ton of money.

You'll find out all about it my boxset: *Apple Cider Vinegar and Baking Soda 101 for Beginners Box Set* by BJ Richards

Check it out here: https://www.amazon.com/Apple-Cider-Vinegar-Baking-Beginners-ebook/dp/B07DPCLWGB/

You can also go **my website** to find even more books I've written and some recommended by other authors: https://bjrichardsauthor.com

Workbook Companion for Girl Stop Apologizing by Rachel Hollis

Made in the USA
Monee, IL
15 November 2020

47851436R00077